CZERNY-GERMER

SELECTED PIANO STUDIES

ARRANGED IN SYSTEMATIC ORDER BY HEINRICH GERMER
EDITED BY WILLARD A. PALMER

50 Short Studies Selected from Opp. 139, 261, 599 and 821
32 Studies Selected from Opp. 335, 636, 829 and 849

Carl Czerny in 1833. *Lithograph by Kriehuber*

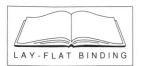

LAY-FLAT BINDING

Alfred has made every effort to make this book not only attractive but more useful and long-lasting as well. Usually, large books do not lie flat or stay open on the music rack. In addition, the pages (which are glued together) tend to break away from the spine after repeated use.

In this edition, pages are sewn together in multiples of 16. This special process prevents pages from falling out of the book while allowing it to stay open for ease in playing. We hope this unique binding will give you added pleasure and additional use.

CONTENTS

PART 1

PART 2

Second Edition

Copyright © MCMXCIII by Alfred Publishing Co., Inc.

All rights reserved.   Printed in USA.

Cover art: The Old Burgtheater in Vienna. *1783*
by Carl Schütz (Austrian, 1745–1800)
Colored etching
Historisches Museum Stadt Wien, Vienna, Austria
Erich Lessing/Art Resource, New York

AN ALFRED MASTERWORK EDITION

FOREWORD

Carl Czerny was born on February 20, 1791, in Vienna, where he died on July 15, 1857. It was a great time and place for a gifted musician, and Czerny made the most of his opportunities to hear most of the legendary masters of the day. He profited greatly from his acquaintance with Hummel and with Clementi, whose method he studied. He was a pupil and confidant of Beethoven, who entrusted to him the musical education of his own nephew when Czerny was only 15 years old. It is easy to be envious of the musical opportunities Czerny enjoyed. How great it must have been to be an important part of the musical scene that included Schubert, Weber, Schumann, Chopin, Liszt, Brahms, Rossini, Paganini, and the many other musical giants of that era! Czerny became one of the most sought-after piano teachers of his day, and numbered among his most famous pupils the great Sigismond Thalberg and the legendary Franz Liszt.

Czerny was a very versatile musician. He was active as a concert artist and was known for his brilliant technique and sensitive playing. As a composer he was incredibly prolific. His compositions include symphonies, concertos, chamber music, 24 masses and many other sacred works, etc., but he owes his lasting fame to his many volumes of piano studies and exercises which have been used for generation after generation by pianists the world over. Because of the demands of publishers for more and more books of exercises, Czerny was forced to write far into the night. He is said to have worked on four or five manuscripts at once, running from one to the other as the ink dried enough for him to turn the pages, meanwhile conversing amiably with anyone who happened to be in the room. His opus numbers run upward to more than 1000. The success of his technical material was due to a few simple facts: they were based on sound knowledge and experience with regard to what is necessary to develop technical facility and accuracy at the keyboard; the themes he employed are generally attractive, and many of the exercises are brilliant enough in their sound to be motivating to play and pleasing to hear. There is also a certain amount of respect due to a musician of Czerny's talents and experience, particularly when we remember that he was a pupil of Beethoven and a teacher of Liszt.

The vast amount of study material left for us by Czerny presents a confusing picture to most piano teachers. Of his technical studies, the following works remain in print to this day: Op. 139, 261, 299, 335, 337, 355, 365, 453, 553, 599, 636, 718, 740, 755, 802, 821, 823, 834, and 849. Each of these volumes contains many exercises; some more than a hundred. It is clearly impossible for aspiring pianists to work on all of these, and it is a difficult task for piano instructors to sort them all out and organize those that might be the most beneficial in a logical and progressive order. This, however, is exactly what Heinrich Germer set out to accomplish. Germer, an outstanding German pianist and pedagogue, was born in Sommerdorf in 1839 and died in Dresden in 1913. He was 18 years old when Czerny died at the age of 66. He had the great opportunity of seeing at first hand the results of Czerny's technical works on the very first generation of pianists who studied them, and he saw the need for reorganization of this vast body of outstanding material. Germer's success is proven by the fact that his systematic organization of the Czerny material, in three volumes, continues to be in great demand by modern piano teachers.

Germer made almost no changes in the actual notes of Czerny's studies. He did add dynamic markings, phrasing and pedaling to make the studies more musical and more satisfying to play. He changed a few antiquated time-signatures to modern ones. He revised Czerny's method of beaming groups of notes to make reading the rhythms much easier. He corrected numerous printing errors. In the longer studies he added capital letters to indicate the beginning of each movement, period or part. This helps the student to determine which portions might best be practiced as a unit in an analytical study of the material. Germer's revisions brought a great deal of order out of chaos, and the results obtained by teachers using them have been gratifying.

ABOUT THE METRONOME INDICATIONS

Czerny indicated metronome tempi for quite a number of his exercises. We have retained them in the present edition, as Germer did in his original publication. Germer himself remarked that it would indeed take a virtuoso to follow these indications, and modern teachers are almost unanimous in their convictions that Czerny's tempi are much too fast. Some have gone so far as to suggest that his metronome may have been in need of adjustment! In any case, there are many benefits to be obtained from these exercises by practicing them slower, and the student who is able to play them well at about 3/4 of the indicated tempi is to be congratulated.

ABOUT THIS NEW EDITION

A new edition of Germer's reorganization of Czerny's studies is long overdue. The previous editor, H. W. Nicholl, may have been a brilliant one, but he had poor proof readers. It is easy enough for typographical errors to escape the eye of editors and publishers in a first printing, but when the same mistakes continue to be printed and reprinted for many, many years, it is inexcusable. In the old printings of the Czerny-Germer studies there are fingering errors, textual mistakes, pedal signs with no indications of release, and releases with no indication of when the pedal was first to be applied. The present editor has attempted to correct all these errors, and has substituted modern pedal marks for the old *Ped.* *. Overlapping pedal is indicated when it is deemed appropriate. Germer expressed his desire to bring Czerny's work ''up to date,'' and would probably agree that a new edition is very much in order. In introducing this one, the present editor will close with one of Germer's own remarks, hoping that ''nothing but the most happy results will follow from its use.''

WILLARD A. PALMER

Part I
50 Short Studies
Selected from Opus 139, 261, 599 and 821

Carl Czerny

TURNS

Allegretto

23

Allegro comodo

Allegro

38

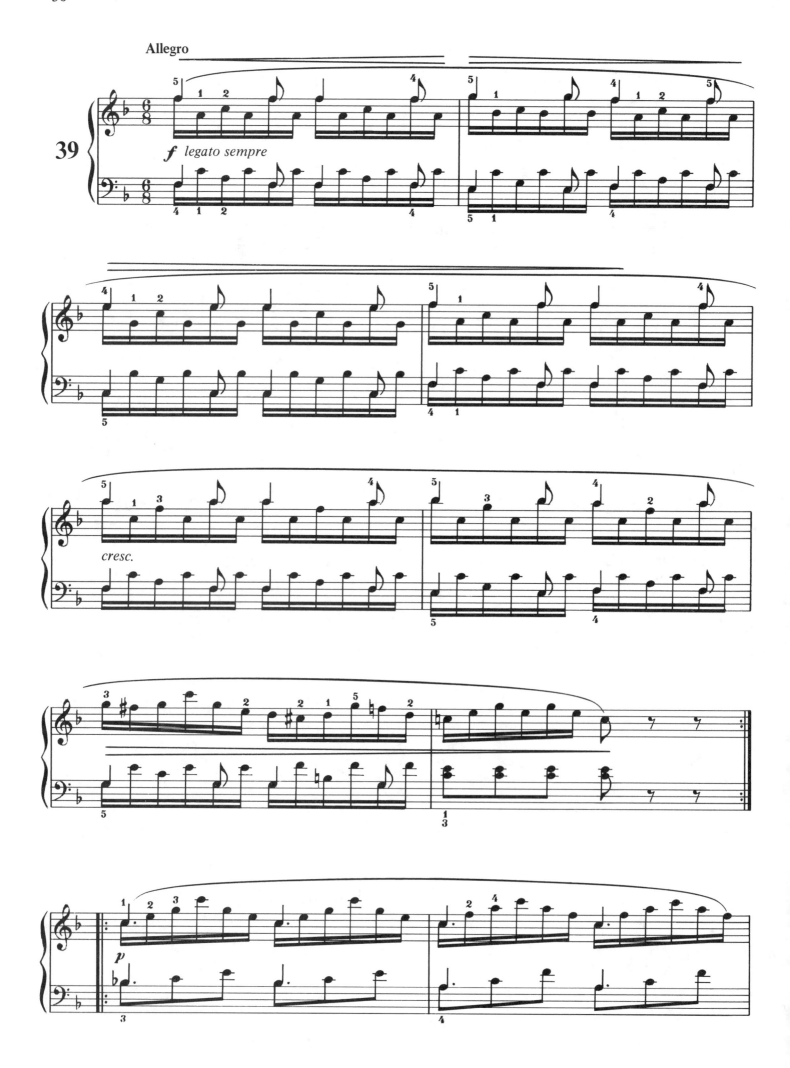

Allegro veloce

49

Part II
32 Studies
Selected from Opus 335, 636, 829 and 849

Carl Czerny

*Czerny indicated metronome tempi for quite a number of his exercises. We have retained them in the present edition, as Germer did in his original publication. Germer himself remarked that it would indeed take a virtuoso to follow these indications, and modern teachers are almost unanimous in their convictions that Czerny's tempi are much too fast. Some have gone so far as to suggest that his metronome may have been in need of adjustment! In any case, there are many benefits to be obtained from these exercises by practicing them slower, and the student who is able to play them well at about 3/4 of the indicated tempi is to be congratulated.

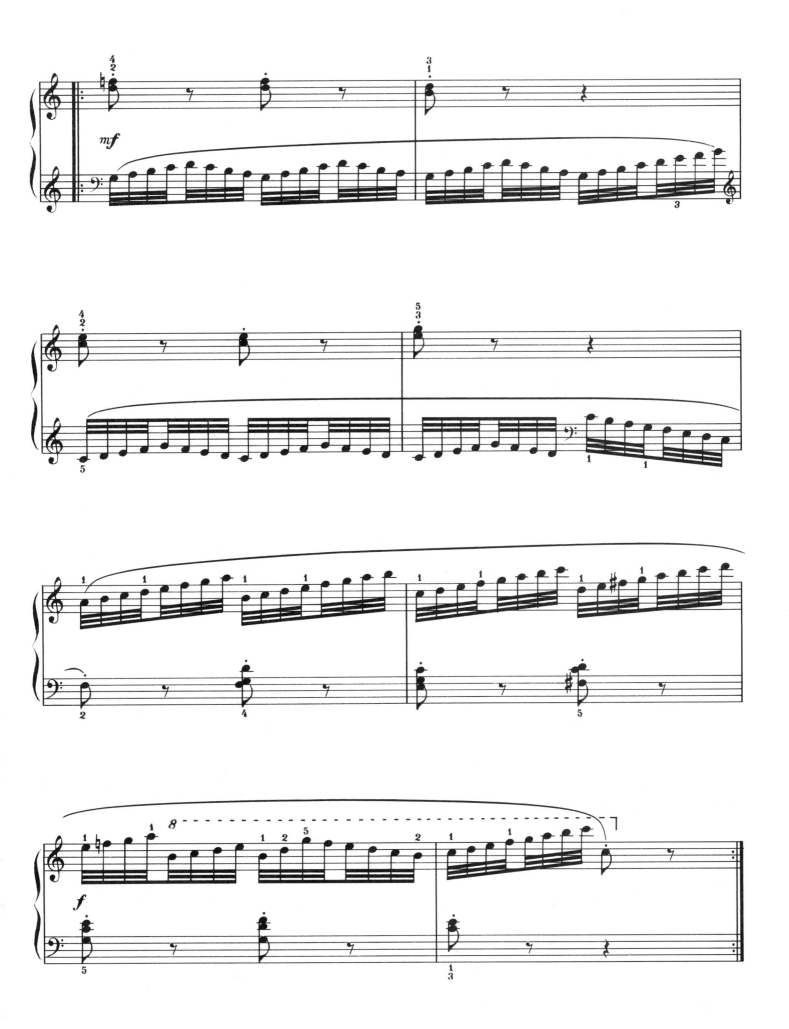

3

Allegro ♩ = 144

p legato

cresc.

f

A

B

p

*Original version:

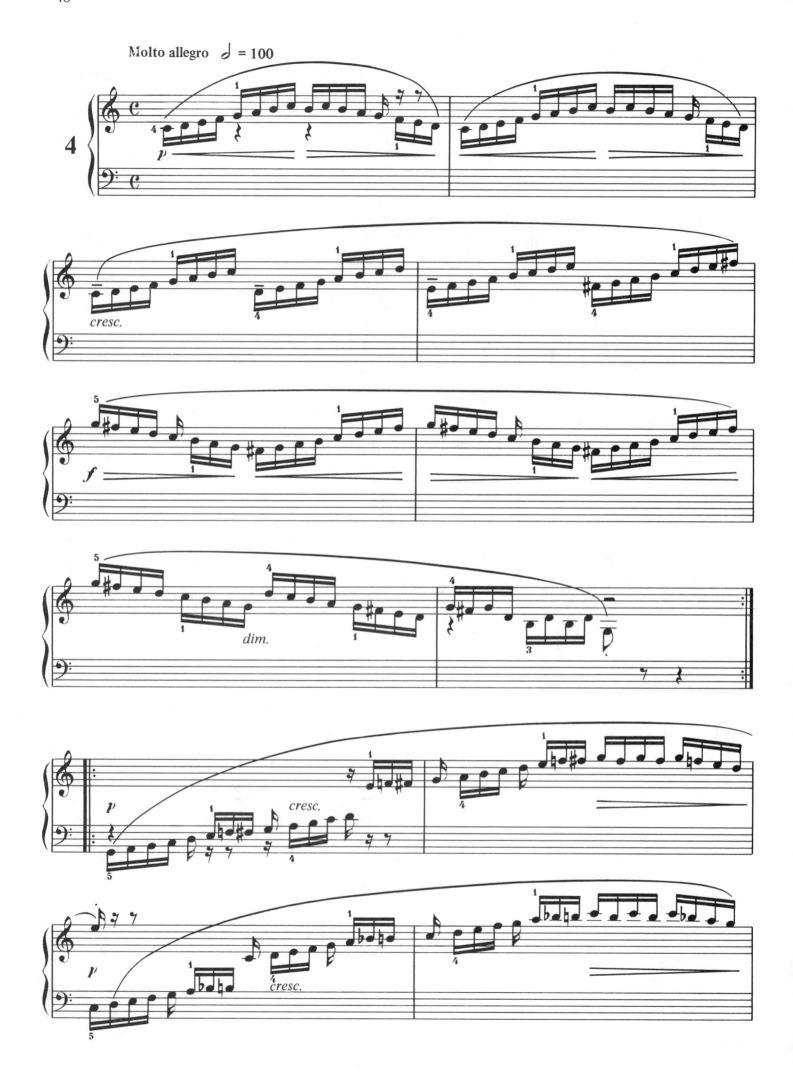

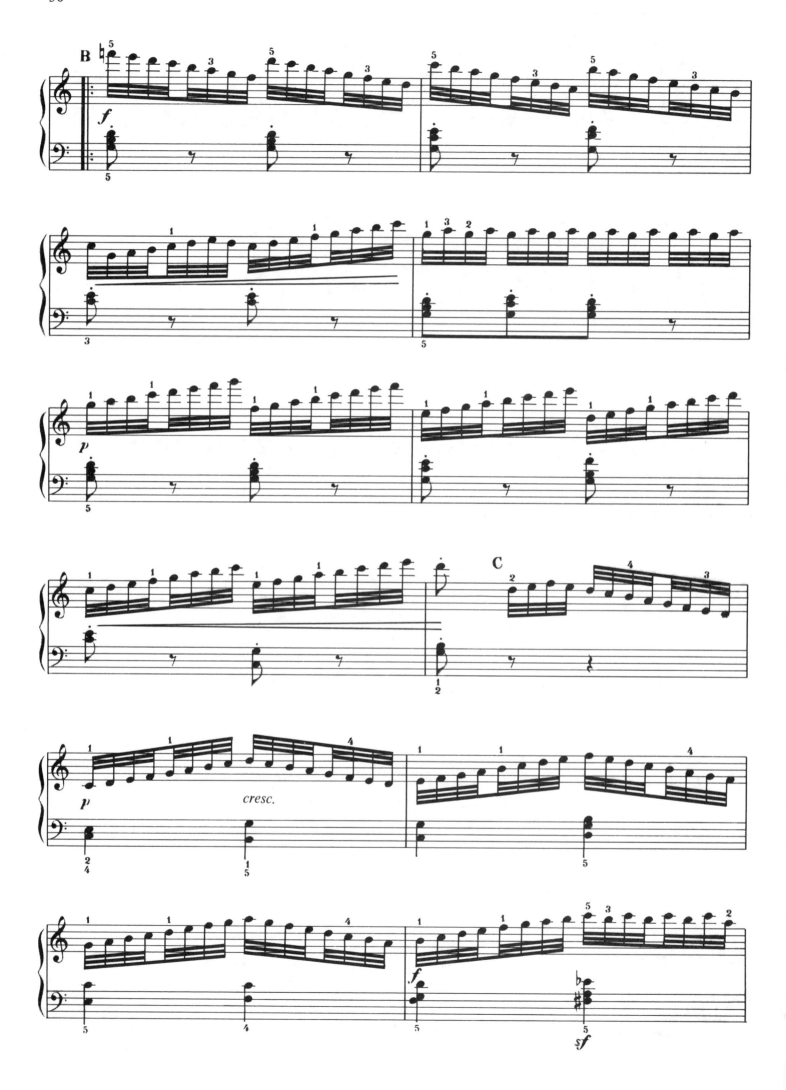

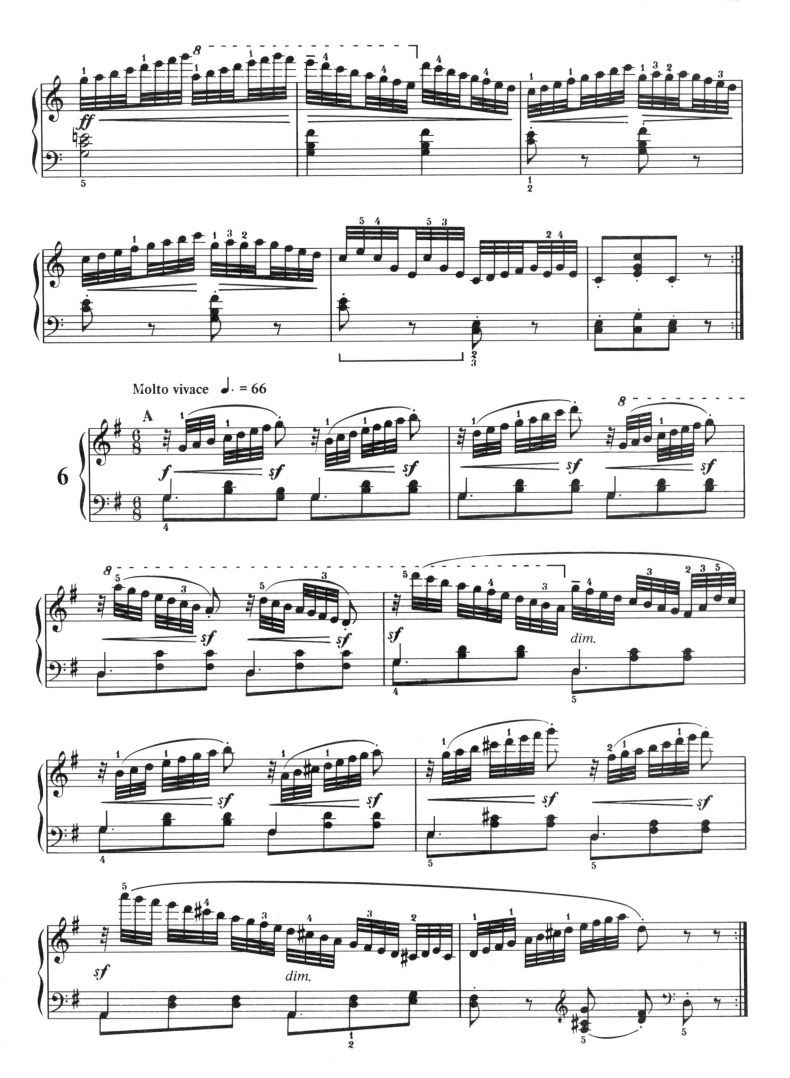

Allegro molto troppo ♩ = 126

Allegro vivo e scherzoso

9

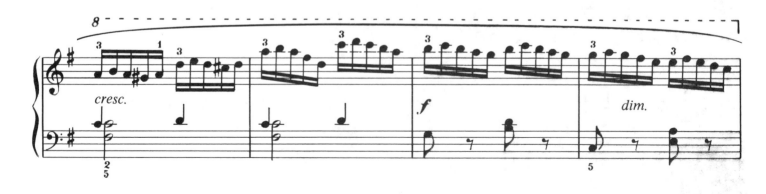

60

Allegro vivo

13

71

Allegro moderato

19

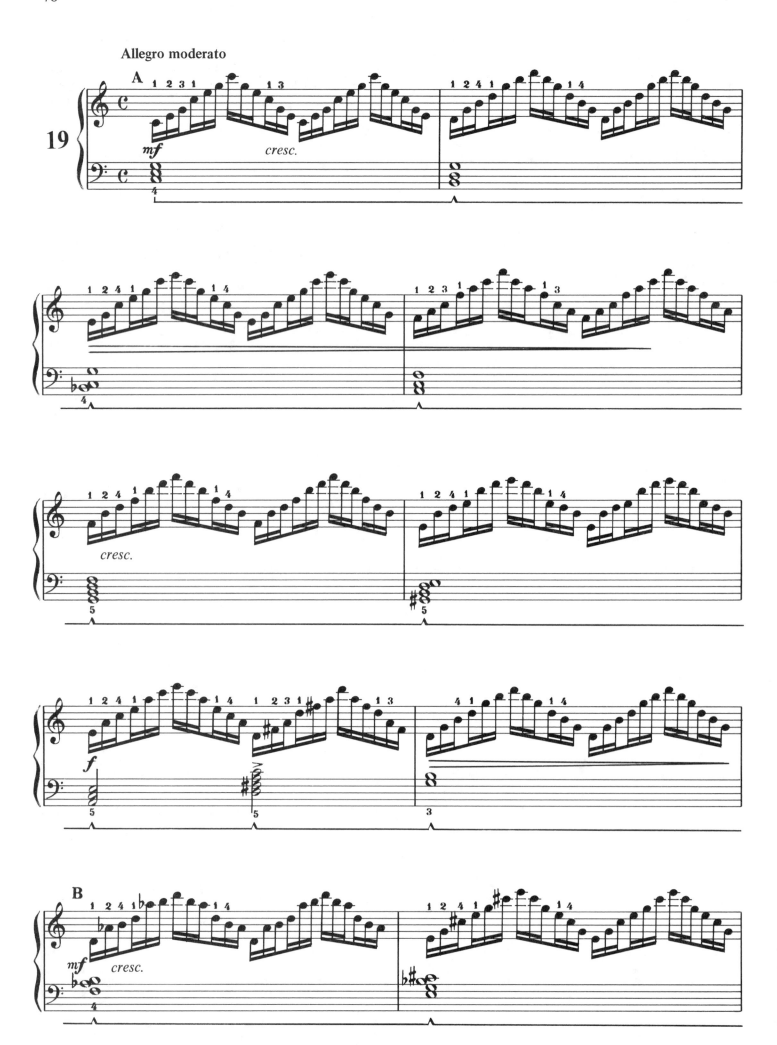

Allegro moderato

20

88

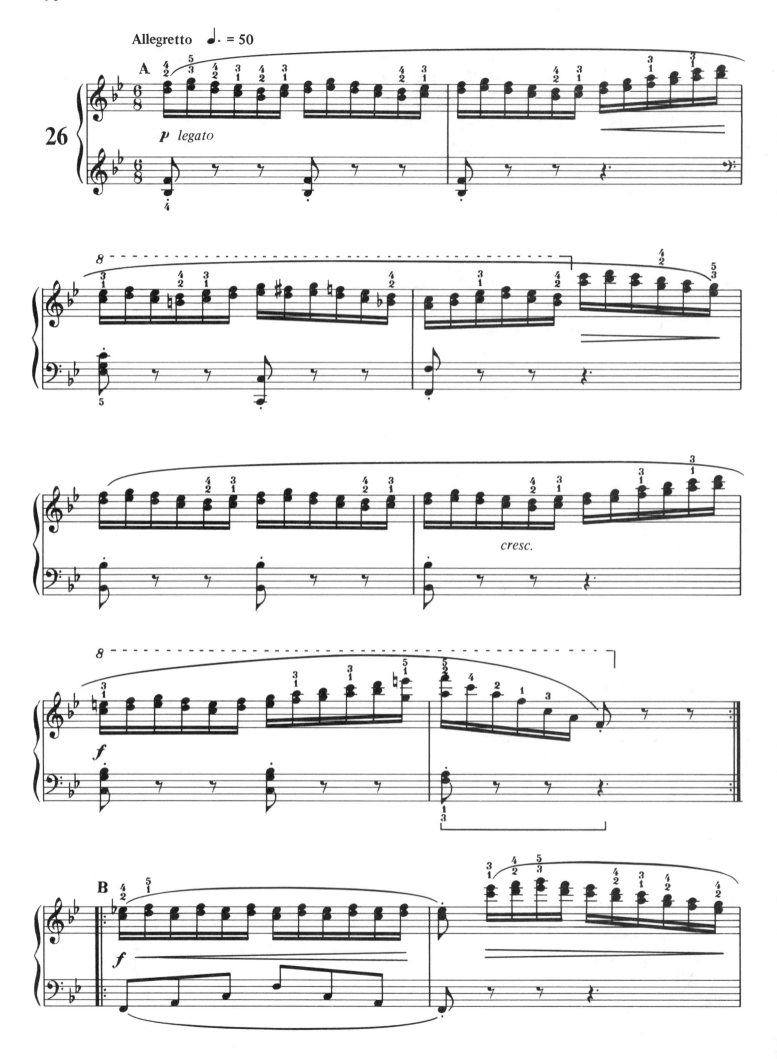

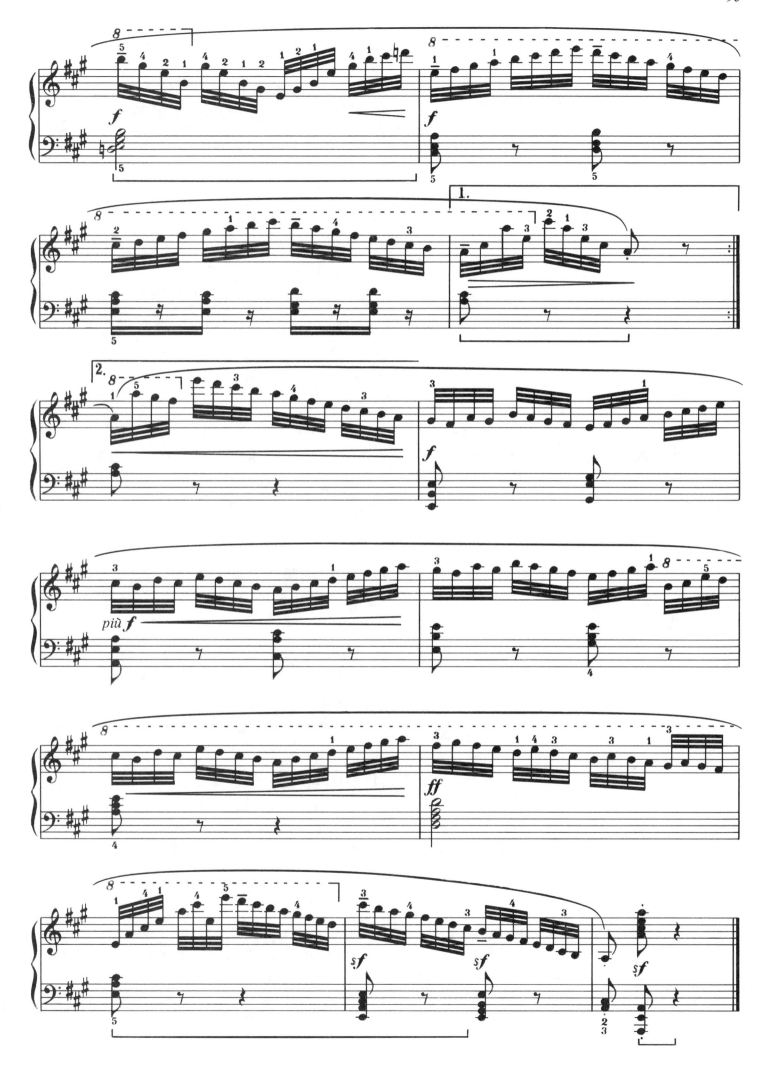

96

Allegro vivace

31